NORDIC TOURING AND CROSS COUNTRY SKIING

M. MICHAEL BRADY

NORDIC
TOURING AND
CROSS COUNTRY
SKIING

THIRD REVISED EDITON

DREYER OSLO, NORWAY

Nordic Touring and Cross Country Skiing
First edition 1966
First edition, second printing 1968
First edition, third printing 1969
Second edition 1970
Second edition, second printing 1971
Copyright © M. Michael Brady 1971, 1970, 1969, 1968, 1966
Third revised edition 1971
Copyright © M. Michael Brady 1971
Library of Congress Catalog Card No. 78-183794

Printed in the United States of America 1971 bv
Port City Press, Inc., New York and Baltimore

PREFACE

This book is devoted to presenting the essentials of Nordic ski touring: a winter activity so diverse in appeal that it can be enjoyed by all.

To the skiing novice, Nordic touring is ideal in that it is basically less expensive, safer, and easier than Alpine downhill skiing to master to the point where it can be enjoyed. There is no "right" age for enjoying Nordic touring. Anyone who walks or hikes can learn the basic walk-like movements and enjoy the freedom of the touring ski.

To the outdoorsman and the mountaineer, Nordic touring is the key to enjoying their activities on a year-round basis. With the proper touring equipment and technique, one can travel much faster than on snowshoes.

To the serious Alpine skier, Nordic ski touring adds a new dimension to the sport. Some of the skiing missed by the skier who does not tour can never be equalled no matter how many downhill runs he makes.

To the athlete, cross-country racing, the competitive form of Nordic touring, is the most comprehensive of all international skiing events. More Winter Olympic gold medals are awarded for cross-country racing than for any other skiing discipline.

To the ski instructor, Nordic ski touring lends itself superbly to instruction, for it builds on what pupils already can do: walk. Nordic touring also offers the professional Alpine ski instructor a recreational outlet; he can escape the slopes by touring.

To the handicapped, Nordic touring skiing is one of the most readily enjoyable and easily learned of winter sports.

The idea for this book was born during the 7th "Interski" — International Ski Instruction Congress — in Badgastein, Austria in January, 1965, and the first edition appeared in January 1966. The second revised edition, reflecting developments in technique and equipment was printed in 1970. Further developments and increased ski touring popularity were the impetus to this third revised and expanded edition. Difference is the theme of this book: only those facets of Nordic ski touring which are *different* from other forms of skiing are presented. Complete descriptions of the myriad of skiing details from underwear to avalanches are left to more pretentious works.

To John Fry and Morten Lund of SKI magazine of New York goes the credit for encouraging and originally publishing much of the material presented here as a series of articles in SKI.

Some of the more important changes made in the second and third editions arose out of discussions with Lorns Olav Skjemstad, who also skied for all the technique sequence photographs of this edition. Six major skiing firms loaned their best in equipment, wax, and clothing for the illustrations. Skiing photographer Frits Solvang's continual cooperation and broad knowledge of the subject are responsible for most of the photographs. Anne McKinnon's constructive, fresh approach to the subject and diligent assistance helped make this third edition possible. And to the many others unnamed here — those who inspired, coached, taught, learned, and raced against — sincere thanks.

M. Michael Brady
Oslo, October 1971

THE DIFFERENCE

...there is a difference

The cat-like grace of the high-speed cross-country racer, the distance-covering, steady stride of polar explorers like Nansen, and the measured, easy pace of a group of school children on a ski tour all share a common skiing technique known as Nordic touring.

Four-thousand-year-old cave wall carvings in arctic Norway attest to the beginnings of an age of skiing which began in and spread out from the Nordic countries. In the latter half of the 19th century "Snowshoe Thompson", from Telemark in Norway, brought skis to California in the U.S., while his countrymen were introducing skiing in central Europe. For many years, the Nordic countries supplied skiing equipment and ski instructors to the world. While the men from the North regarded skis as an integral part of life itself, central Europeans and Americans began skiing for sport and recreation. In the years that followed, the central Europeans developed their own form for pleasure skiing, suited to their steep Alpine slopes, while their Nordic teachers retained their traditional form of skiing. Thus today one speaks of Nordic and Alpine skiing as two forms of skiing that have become considerably different in purpose, technique, and equipment. Nordic skiing comprises Nordic touring, cross-country racing, and jumping, while Alpine skiing comprises recreational downhill skiing and the slalom and downhill racing events.

Most Americans, Canadians, Englishmen, Australians, and Central Europeans are familiar only with the specialized branch of skiing known as *Alpine* skiing. Alpine skiing equipment is designed for downhill use only; the weight of the skis (5.0 kg or 11 lbs for an average pair of metal skis), the stiff, reinforced boots with their steel-shanked soles, and the rigid bindings make lifts desirable, if not necessary. In countries where Alpine skiing prevails, climbing uphill with skins attached to Alpine skis to get a good downhill run is sometimes known as "touring".

True Nordic touring is not an uphill trek with skins fastened to heavy skis just for the sake of a downhill run. Nordic touring skis can be used anywhere there is snow. The expanse of mountain glaciers and the stillness of snow-covered frozen lakes are not simply temptations, but are the realm of the Nordic touring skier. A ski trail offers its own particular challenge, snaking

The start of Sweden's Vasaloppet race

through woods, it may rise evenly, or drop suddenly for a challenging slalom run between the trees. The touring skier is never snowbound, snow-closed roads cannot prevent him from enjoying the quiet of an isolated mountain cabin, or discovering the beauty of a mountain valley in its winter setting. Even a city park becomes a ski area for the touring skier. To the cross-country racer, the challenge of pitting his experience and ability against terrain and the clock is a calling all its own.

Nordic touring is the most common form of skiing in the Scandinavian countries. The skis used are thinner and lighter than Alpine skis. Boots are simple, and are fastened to toe pieces, and the heel is completely free to lift off the ski. As opposed to the downhill-only nature of Alpine equipment and technique, Nordic equipment and technique are intended to be used uphill, downhill, on the flat - *everywhere*.

Cross-country racing, which is known as "Langlauf" in German, and "langrenn" in Norwegian, is a ski race run with extremely light skis (1.2 kg or 2-lb, 11-oz for an average pair of racing skis) fastened only at the extreme tip of the toe of a boot that resembles an ordinary shoe. As an athletic performance. it is similar to a marathon race, the standard distances being from 5 kilometers (3 miles) to 50 kilometers (31 miles). The pace is fast, with usual times over international-standard 15 km courses being about 50 minutes, and about 2 hours and 45 minutes for 50-km courses.

In the Scandinavian countries, Nordic touring is, and always has been, an integral part of life. Pleasure touring, cross-country racing, and national history blend into one another until it is sometimes difficult to tell which is which. Each winter, touring races - endurance events divided into classes for cross-country racers and ordinary touring skiers - are run in Norway, Sweden, and Finland. Some of these races have their beginnings rooted in history. Sweden's Vasaloppet can well claim to be the world's largest ski race. It follows the route skied from Sälen to Mora in 1521 by the Swedish patriot Gustaf Vasa, and is 85.5 km (53 miles) long. Eight to ten thousand skiers annually enter the Vasaloppet, and the best time yet over the route was set in 1961 at 4 hours, 45 minutes and 10 seconds: an average of 3 min, 21 sec per kilometer (or 5 min, 23 sec per mile). Although originally Scandinavian, touring races are no longer limited to Scandinavia; even in some Alpine countries, touring races have become the most popular form of competition for recreational skiers. The Paddy Pallin race in Australia and the Washington's Birthday race in the United States annually draw hundreds of starters. Touring races in major European Alpine ski areas draw international participation, and the «Volkslanglauf» races in Germany often have over a thousand starters.

There are hundreds of cross-country races each year in Scandinavia; in Finland there are over 4000 cross-country and touring race events each winter. Even the prestigious Winter Olympics has more cross-country racing events than any other ski event: there are four men's and three women's cross-country events plus two in biathlon (cross-country skiing and shooting) and the Nordic combined (cross-country skiing and ski jumping). Alpine skiing is next on the list, with a total of six events.

Nordic skiing also includes ski jumping, which is a competitive event rarely done for recreation. The skis used are longer and wider than any other type of ski, and have three to five tracking grooves instead of one. The boots are cut low with a built-in forward lean, and are fixed to the ski with a toe iron and heel cable, such that the heel is free to lift off the ski.

There is a difference between Nordic ski touring and all other forms of skiing: pleasure and competitive Alpine skiing and Nordic ski jumping. *This is a book about this difference.*

TECHNIQUE

Competition technique is best (Gerhard Grimmer, first place 1971 Holmenkollen 50 km)

The movements of Nordic touring are not difficult to learn, because its movements are an extension of something everyone can do: walk.

The basic term in touring technique is the "diagonal stride". It means that you use the opposite arm and leg together just like walking. The arm plants the pole while the opposite leg pushes off or "kicks". The diagonal stride can be best learned by starting with an ordinary walking stride on skis. The force of the walking kick is progressively increased, the upper body

14

bends more forward, and the arms swing more to produce the correct diagonal stride. Just as in walking, the effect of the kick is to propel the skier forward. The pole helps in this maneuver, supplying from as little as a tenth up to a quarter of the energy to drive the skier forward.

The movements of the diagonal stride resemble an exaggerated march step, as opposing arm and leg work together.

The mark of a skilled touring skier is a relaxed, easy stride, with rapid pushing movements, plus long glides with the weight balanced on one ski or the other. Other than tempo, there is little difference between *good* Nordic touring technique and *good* cross-country racing technique. The racer wants to eliminate all energy-wasting movements so he can go faster over longer periods of time. The same elimination of energy-wasting movements minimize fatigue for the touring skier. As in most other physical activities, the technique of the top competitors is the

Other than tempo, there is little difference between good Nordic touring technique and good cross-country racing technique.

An ordinary walking stride can be done on skis.

best technique: it is efficient, rhythmic, and natural. You should be able to tour using far less energy than in hiking over the same terrain. One of the best tricks is to relax the head and shoulders by focusing your eyes about 10 to 15 meters (about 40 feet) ahead of you; continual watching of your ski tips will result in a cramped and tiring position.

The diagonal stride uses the principles of ice and roller skating. In ice skating you glide on alternate skates and obtain forward drive by kicking off a weighted blade which is slightly angled to your direction of motion. In skating, the "kicking leg" swings backwards after the kick-off. The other leg gets the weight, and gives a push in its turn. The skating stride is then a kick-glide, kick-glide stride. To pick up speed in skating, side-to-side arm movements are added to counterbalance the kicking leg. Those rhythmical kick-and-glide movements are analogous to the touring stride illustrated on the following pages.

Leaning a bit more forward   and kicking harder turns it into the
diagonal ski stride.

For going uphill, the basic diagonal stride is modified slightly, and becomes the uphill diagonal stride. To provide variation and a rest from the kicking of the diagonal stride, both poles can be set simultaneously in "double poling", to push the body forward. The diagonal stride and double-poling can be supplanted by the "double-pole" stride, wich uses some movements from each.

If you are accustomed to Alpine skis, it may seem quite a mystery that the same ski surface can be used both to grip and then glide. The action of touring ski wax on snow is very much like a stiff brush on a wet boat deck. If you strapped brushes on your feet, you could kick off from one, and yet slide forward on the other. The basic principle applies to skis. A ski will glide as long as it is in motion. Once gliding stops, it will stick until it is picked up slightly so it can glide again.

DIAGONAL STRIDE

The right leg is even with the left, which is now weighted. With a slight, rapid sinking in its knee, the left leg starts its backward kick. The right arm has started its push just before the left leg's kick.

The left leg has almost completed its kick; a gradual weight shift to the right leg starts. The right arm has finished its pole push. The left arm has almost completed its forward swing.

This is gliding: the right leg is now carrying all weight. The right arm has begun to swing forward, and the left pole is just being planted. Note the bend of the gliding knee and ankle.

The left leg n swings forward; i still unweighted. T right arm swin forward, while left arm exe downward force its pole.

The illustrations show two complete paces of the diagonal stride. In the first four figures, the right leg and left arm are forward. In the last three figures, the left leg and right arm are forward. This is what is meant by diagonal — the diagonally opposite limbs follow one another in their forward and back movements.

Note that the head and shoulders stay relatively fixed, and do not bob up and down, or from side to side. Vertical or

18

The left leg is even with the right, which **now** is weighted. This phase of the stride is just opposite to that of the first picture. The right leg starts its backward kick and the left arm has started its push.

The right leg has almost completed its kick. This phase of the stride is opposite to that of the second picture. The left arm has almost completed its pole push. The right arm has almost come completely forward.

This is gliding on the left ski, just the opposite phase to the third picture. The left arm has begun to swing forward, and the right pole is just being planted.

side to side motion does not push you forward and should be eliminated as much as possible.

If you have trouble coordinating your arm and leg movements, practice skiing the diagonal stride without poles.

In this and all the touring strides, the hand grip used on the poles is important. The correct grip sequence allows full relaxation and extension of the arms. Gripping the poles too tightly will restrict pole movement and tire you out quickly.

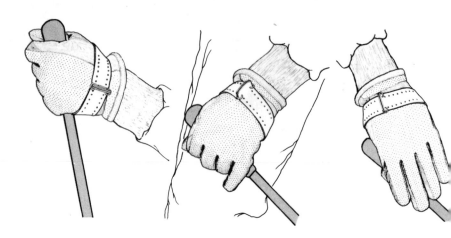

When the poles are planted in front of the body, the hand grip should be closed but relaxed.

As the pole and arm pass the body, the grip should begin to loosen.

When the arm is completely in back of the body, the grip should be relaxed, and the pole held loosely between thumb and fingers.

DOUBLE POLING

Both poles can be set simultaneously to provide variation in movement, or to increase speed under good conditions or on downhill stretches. Double-poling can be used with or without strides between successive double-poles. On the flat, or under resistant snow conditions, double-poling takes a good deal more energy than does the diagonal stride. Thus it cannot be maintained for long periods of time. In double-poling, the upper body goes forward to throw weight onto the poles after they are planted. This used body weight, and not merely arm muscle gives the movement its power. Because the speed in double-poling is greater, the poles are set with their baskets further forward than for the diagonal stride, with shafts almost vertical. The sequence figures on pages 22-23 show one complete double-pole maneuver.

DOUBLE-POLE STRIDE

The arm movements of double-poling and the leg movements of the diagonal stride can be combined to form a third stride, the "double-pole stride." Like double poling, the double-pole stride uses more energy than the diagonal stride and can not be used over very long distances without being tiring. But, like double-poling and the diagonal stride, it is efficient when done correctly. It can easily be done even with a rucksack on your back, as shown by the sequence pictures on pages 22-23. The basic double pole stride can be modified by taking two complete kick-and-glide paces on alternate legs instead of one in between successive pole plantings. Arms keep the same movements, but there are two complete leg strides between the second and sixth pictures.

A relaxed and rhythmical diagonal stride is the secret to all Nordic touring and cross-country skiing (skiing in Nordmarka, Oslo, Norway).

DOUBLE POLING

The poles are set with the arms bent slightly. The upper body arches over and to weight the poles.

The body sinks smoothly and continuously over the poles. Only now do the arms start to push backwards.

The arms now push past the knees with hands almost touching and level with, or a little below, the knees.

DOUBLE-POLE STRIDE

The skier is gliding with skis equally weighted, and body relaxed.

Both arms swing forward. The right leg is weighted and kicking backwards.

The right leg kick is complete, and the skier is gliding on his left ski. The skier stretches well forward to get the most out of the pole plant.

The poles ha been planted, a right leg is forward. The starts to sink o poles.

The push move-
ment ends, and the
skier is gliding on
equally weighted
skis.

The arms now
swing forward to
prepare for the next
pole set as the body
straightens.

The poles are now
set again for another
poling movement.

The right leg has
almost completed
its forward swing,
and the skier sinks
over his poles.

The skier sinks
further over his
poles, with hands
at about knee level,
and starts pushing
backwards.

The skier glides
on equally weighted
skis as the arms
swing up in back
and the body
straightens.

CHANGING STRIDES

There is no one set method of changing from diagonal stride to double poling or vice versa; individual skiers use individual motions in order to maintain rhythm. To change from the diagonal stride to double-poling, a half pole movement can be taken from the first or fifth positions of the diagonal stride sequence; thus puts the skier in the first position of double-poling. Another commonly used method is to skip a pole setting and hold the forward arm fixed until the opposing arm swings forward; thus puts the skier in the second position of the double-poling. Shifting from double-poling to the diagonal stride is similar to the first three figures of the double-pole stride sequence except that only one arm is swung forward. This puts the skier in the second or seventh positions of the diagonal stride.

CHANGING DIRECTION FROM A STANDSTILL

There are a number of ways to change direction on flat or gently sloping terrain. The simplest is to shuffle progressively around, first picking up one ski and angling it slightly towards the new direction, bringing the other ski parallel, and then repeating the movements until facing the new direction. The kick turn shown here requires a bit more balance, but is definitely quicker and can be done on steep hillsides.

FLAT TERRAIN TURNS

Turns are changes in direction, made while in motion. The most commonly used ski touring turn for flat or gently sloping terrain is the skating turn shown on p. 26. The skating turn allows you to maintain, and often increase your speed, while changing direction. This advantage, combined with the ease with which it fits into the diagonal stride and double-poling rhythms, makes the skating turn the most used. A good diagonal stride and a good skating turn are often considered the keys to mastering ski touring technique.

Beginning and ending a skating turn with a double-poling gives greater balance and power. The first figure of the skating turn sequence is a front view of the final position of the double-poling sequence, and the last position is equivalent to the first position of the double-poling sequence.

KICK TURN

Skis are parallel and equally weighted, poles in front and unweighted.

The "inside" pole is planted near the tail of the ski, weight remaining equally distributed on both poles for balance.

The inside ski is kicked up and forward. Pivoting the ski, the tip is brought down in the opposite direction.

The inside ski is now flat on the snow in the new direction. Weight is transferred to this ski and its pole.

The outside ski and pole are now brought around. The position is now the same as the first but the direction is reversed.

SKATING TURN

This is the final phase of ▶ double poling. Body weight starts to shift to the outside (left) ski.

The outside ski is completely weighted and the inside ski is unweighted, lifted off the snow, and pointing in the new direction. The body is in a crouch and the arms are drawn back: the skier is "coiled" for the spring. ▶

▲

With a quick kick on the outside leg, and a forward thrust of the upper body, the skier springs onto the inside ski in the new direction. Weight is completely on the inside ski, which is gliding in the new direction.

▲

The outside leg swings down with its ski parallel to the inside ski. Both skis will now be weighted, and the skier will glide in the new direction. The arms swing forward for another double poling.

UPHILL TECHNIQUE

Skiing uphill requires better technique than any other part of touring and cross-country skiing. Poor uphill technique is slow and tiring; bad uphill technique lets you slide back downhill. Thus it is often said that cross-country races are won or lost on the uphill stretches. For slight inclines, the diagonal stride can be used directly, with a shortening of its gliding phase. For steeper inclines, an uphill modification of the diagonal stride is used.

The major outward difference in using the diagonal stride in level terrain and up an incline is that the characteristic gliding phase becomes shorter as the incline becomes steeper. To maintain any forward speed at all, more powerful, and shorter movements of arms an legs are necessary. The kick from a seemingly flat foot is gone, and the skier must literally be on his toes, springing from his ankles to push down as well as forward. This movement is not only technically correct, but also helps "set" wax, or make it hold on the hill. These differences make the uphill stride seem like jogging. The three sequences shown on p. 28 illustrate these differences. Compare them with the corresponding phases of the diagonal stride.

The differences between the uphill and flat-terrain diagonal strides are then:

1) The glide phase is shorter
2) The gliding knee is over the foot.
   This characteristic position is what keeps the ski from slipping backwards downhill.
3) Knees and elbows bend more to compensate for the incline.
4) Pole pushing movements are shorter.
5) The skier is more on his toes.
6) There may not be enough time or distance for complete extension of the arms.

When the slope is too steep to use the direct-uphill diagonal stride, you can use the familiar herringbone uphill step. For still steeper inclines, upward traversing combined with rhythmic step-turning or "tacking" may be used. Both these techniques use the basic arm and leg movements of the diagonal stride. These strides are illustrated on the next two pages.

UPHILL STRIDE

The left leg kick is nearly finished. Note that the waist, knees, and ankles are bent more than the corresponding position in the diagonal stride. Note that the right knee is directly over the right foot.

HERRINGBONE

The skis are in the herringbone position, opened in a wide, forward Vee. The skier has just completed a kick on his left ski and a push on his right pole. The right leg is swung forward, and the left pole is swung forward ready for the plant.

This is the intermediate position; the right leg has just started its kick. Note that the skier is on his left toes. In the corresponding position of the diagonal stride (the fifth picture), the skier's left foot was flat on its ski. Both knees and elbows are bent more than in the flat-terrain diagonal stride, to provide the little extra muscle force to maintain uphill glide.

The right leg fully extended and i͏ kick is finished; th͏ weight now transfe͏ to the left ski. The rig͏ arm is pulling. Th͏ left knee is verticall͏ over the left foot.

This is the opposite p͏ to the first picture. The sk͏ almost completed the k͏ his right leg and the pu͏ his left pole. The left l͏ right pole are swinging f͏

TACKING

5. Without moving either pole, the skier kicks from his uphill (right) ski, taking half a diagonal stride. He then resumes the diagonal stride in the new direction.

4. Now, with a single thrusting-extending of the right arm and leg, the skier swings the right ski and pole up, around, and parallel to the left ski. The pole is being planted just behind the right foot to secure the ski.

3. The skier swings his uphill (left) ski up, forward, and around to point in the new traverse direction. The left pole is planted just behind the left foot and held firmly to prevent slipping downhill.

2. The glide has just been completed on the downhill (right) ski and the skier starts the tack by planting the right pole near the right foot and crouching much as one does in starting the skating turn.

he skier is on a tra-se, skiing uphill using diagonal stride.

DOWNHILL RUNNING AND TURNS

Approximately half of the world's skiing literature is devoted to downhill running and turns. No attempt will be made here to describe the fine points and various ski school techniques described in such infinite detail elsewhere. Like the rest of ski touring technique, downhill touring technique should be simple and efficient.

The rigid Alpine ski-binding-boot combination is designed to transmit every fine leg movement to the skis. Although some touring bindings have attachments to help hold the heels down for downhill runs, the greater freedom and flexibility of touring boots, bindings, and skis means that the whole body is more obviously used than in the corresponding Alpine techniques.

Man is by nature a biped, and ski touring is a biped activity. Hence, it is both technically and physiologically correct for the touring skier to assume the wide-track (skis apart) position in all downhill technique. The wide-track position is the natural position of readiness and balance.

The downhill running stances used in ski touring are the same as those used in Alpine skiing. They vary from the more erect, natural athletic stance, to the high-speed egg position. The four most common positions are shown here along with the downhill snowplow.

The flat-terrain skating turn can be used on moderate slopes, whereas stem turns or stem Christianias can be done on almost any skiable slope. The sequence pictures on p. 32 show the phases of a stem turn to the right. More expert touring skiers and top cross-country racers can even do tightly linked parallel turns with the lightest of cross-country racing equipment. The sequence pictures on p. 33 show one turn of a Wedeln series. The older Telemark turn for deep snow is very seldom seen in modern ski touring. The stem turn is the most-used standard downhill touring turn.

DOWNHILL

The basic wide-track downhill position. Ankles, knees, and hips are slightly bent, and these together with leg and lower back muscles supply balance.

A stabler position for the touring skier. Ankles, knees, and hips are bent more. The position is one of readiness. The knees are bent in a supple action to absorb bumps, changes in slope, or transitions to patches of sticky snow.

A high crouch or partial egg position, as often used by cross-country racers, and some touring skiers. Wind resistance is less than in either of the previous two positions, yet the stability is high. This position is preferred to the full egg when the terrain demands fast changes of position.

The full egg position used in racing. The skier has a compact, streamlined position and the balance of the wide-track stance. However, the stability is not as high as that of the partial egg position; its compactness makes it hard to respond rapidly, or absorb great shocks.

The downhill snowplow can be used to regain balance, slow down, stop, or initiate a lower-speed turn.

STEM TURN

The skier is skiing on a downhill traverse in a wide-track position. Note the relaxed bend in the ankles, knees and hips.

With weight mostly on the downhill (right) ski, the skier stems his uphill (left) ski out to point in the direction of the turn. Note that the body stance is still squarely over the skis.

The skier weights the outside ski to start the turn. The inside (right) ski is almost completely unweighted. The body is squarely over the skis.

The weight is still on the outside ski as the skis come around to the new direction. The inside ski is still unweighted and begins to close in parallel to the outside ski.

The inside ski is now almost parallel with the outside ski and the skier is again skiing on a downhill traverse in the wide-track position.

32

WEDELN

The skier is on a downhill traverse in a wide track position and is preparing to plant his inside (left) pole. Ankles, knees, and hips are bent for a slightly deeper stance than used in the stem turn.

The skier moves up as e weights his outside ght) ski and plants his side pole to initiate the rallel turn. Note that e inside ski is completely weighted.

The skis are now pointing in the new direction. ankles, and hips more, to side slip the skis around to the new direction. Note that the body is squarely over the skis.

The skis are now pointing in the new direction. This is the opposite of the first picture; the skier is now preparing to make a turn to the right.

SKIS, BOOTS, BINDINGS, AND POLES

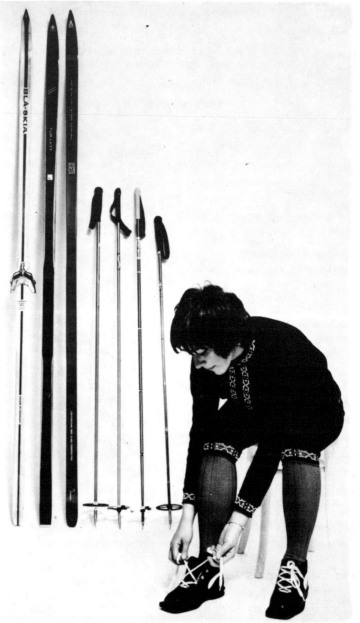

Skis, boots, bindings, and poles — the necessities of the sport.

The different forms of Nordic skiing require equipment which varies in characteristics and construction according to intended use. There are three distinct types of pleasure touring: mountain, general, and light. Cross-country racing is the competitive form of Nordic touring. The equipment used by the mountain skier, who must carry a heavy rucksack under varying snow and slope conditions for tours which may last several days to several weeks, is understandably different from that used by a cross-country racer, who attempts to maintain the highest possible speed over a prepared ski track, for a period of time which seldom exceeds three hours. Mountain- and cross-country equipment represent the heavy and light extremes of Nordic equipment as it is known today. General- and light-touring equipment then fill out the list of the four categories of equipment. Although these four categories are individually different, the characteristics of lightest weight for a given strength, and greatest durability for a given use are common throughout.

The weights and major dimensions of the various types of Nordic skis, boots, and bindings are compared against Alpine equipment in the table on page 36. A quick glance at the weights will reveal the secret behind the light stride of the cross-country racer; he carries over 8 kg (about 17½ pounds) less on his feet than does the slalom skier. The old adage that "a pound on your feet is like five on your back" well describes the penalty paid in effort for heavy equipment; the cross-country racer is carrying over 40 kg (about 88 pounds) *less* equivalent weight on his back.

SKIS

The four types of Nordic ski are compared against a typical Alpine ski on page 37. Unlike the metal Alpine ski illustrated, the Nordic skis are made of wood, or wood reinforced with fiberglass. As this third edition goes to press, a few successful models of synthetic-material light-touring and cross-country racing skis have been placed on the market. But for the vast majority of present-day Nordic skis, the desired ski characteristics, lightness, and wax-holding ability are achieved by a laminated wood construction as shown on page 38.

35

Skis
Example: 205 cm (6 foot, 9 inch) skis

Boots
Example: Men's 41 (US:9)

Type	Skis			Boots		Bindings		Total weight of skis, boots and bindings
	Edges	Max. width	Pair weight	Features	Pair weight	Type	Pair weight	
Special Cross-Country Racing	hardwood or plastic	5.2 cm 2-1/16 in.	1.2-1.4 kg 2 lb 11 oz.	light, flexible cut below ankle resemble ordinary shoes	740 gr 1 lb 10 oz	cross-country toe clamp	125 gr 5 oz	2.07 - 2.27 kg 4 lb 10 oz - 5 lb
Cross-Country Racing	hardwood, plastic, or compressed hardwood	5.9 cm 2-5/16 in.	1.7 kg 3 lb 12 oz.					2.57 kg 5 lb 11 oz
Light Touring	compressed hardwood, or plastic	6.5 cm 2-9/16 in.	2.0 kg 4 lb. 7 oz.	Similar to above, cut above ankle	920 gr 2 lb			3.05 kg 6 lb 12 oz
General Touring	compressed hardwood, plastic, or aluminum	7.3 cm 3 in.	2.5 kg 5 lb 8 oz.	resembles hiking boot	1.62 kg 3 lb 9 oz	toe-iron with heelcable or band	955 gr 2 lb 2 oz	5.08 kg 11 lb 3 oz
Mountain	compressed hardwood or steel	8 cm 3-1/8 in.	3.0 kg 6 lb 10 oz.					5.58 kg 12 lb 5 oz
Alpine fiberglass	steel	8.8 cm 3-7/16 in.	4.54 kg 10 lb.	double, plastic with buckles	4.0 kg 8 lb 13 oz	toe-release with heel release	1.25 kg 2 lb 13 oz	9.79 kg 21 lb 10 oz
Alpine metal	steel	8.5 cm 3-3/4 in	5.0 kg 11 lb.					10.25 kg 22 lb 10 oz

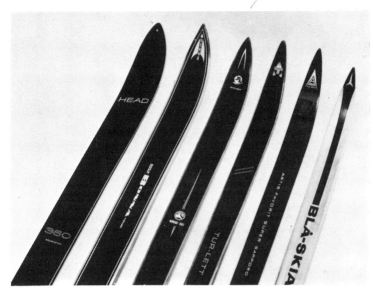

From left to right: metal Alpine ski (Head, USA), Mountain ski (Bonna, Norway), Touring Ski (Trysil Knut, Norway), Light Touring Ski (Toppen, Norway), Fiberglass Light Touring Ski (Artis, Czechoslovakia), and Cross-Country Racing Ski (Blå Skia, Norway).

Nordic skis may use as many as 32 individual laminations in a built-up construction. Spruce is almost universally used for the mid-section, while birch, beech, hickory, and ash are used for the side and top laminations. Thus far, no synthetic material has been marketed which will take and hold touring waxes as well as treated wood. Conversely, no touring waxes have been developed to adhere as well to present synthetic materials as they do to wood. However, some synthetic running surfaces have been developed and skied with promising results. Some of the experimental plastic surfaces seem to hold wax as well as wood for certain temperature ranges. Experiments with "wax-less" skis having serrated or fish-scale running surface have also shown some promise. But at the present time, the running surfaces of the majority of modern Nordic skis are made of either birch or hickory wood. As shown on page 38, even some fiberglass touring skis have a wood running surface. Both birch and hickory are sufficiently strong for running surface laminations, but birch holds touring wax much better and is much

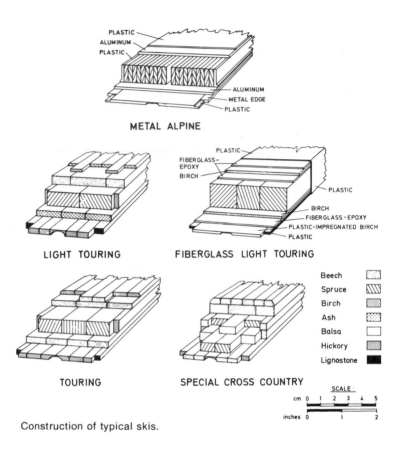

Construction of typical skis.

lighter, though less durable than hickory. Hickory and "Lignostone" (From the Latin: "Lignum" meaning wood), which is beech wood compressed in a resin impregnating process to one-half its original volume, are used for edges. Some ski models are available with glued-on aluminum or plastic edges.

Like Alpine skis. Nordic skis are side-cambered to aid tracking. Except for mountain skis, they have extremely soft tips and slightly harder tails. This combination of tension allows a ski tip to follow small terrain variations, while giving the ski a "forward spring" characteristic. Forward spring is perhaps the major mechanical difference between Nordic skis and other skis. To understand forward spring, picture a ski lying parallel to a floor supported only under its tip and tail by 2-cm (about 3/4 inch) thick books. Now if the center of the ski is weighted such that it bends down and touches the floor, and the ski has an equally-stiff tip and tail, it will have equal spring in both ends. When suddenly unweighted, it will spring vertically up in the air. On the other hand, a ski having a soft tip and a slightly stiffer tail will spring upward and forward, under the same conditions. This upward and forward motion is known as "forward spring", and gives a little extra forward push which makes touring strides easier.

Camber and total ski stiffness should be selected to match a skier's weight and touring style. Generally, the camber and stiffness should be large enough to just flatten the ski's running surface when the ski is weighted with the entire body weight. Too stiff a ski will not contact the snow over its entire running surface, and will lose the benefit of any wax used. Too weak a ski will turn up at the tip and tail and will not track well.

Cross-country Racing Skis are the lightest and most lively of all Nordic skis. Light woods such as birch and beech are used in the side and top laminations, while birch is used in the running-surface laminations and hickory or plastic is used for edges. The most recent development in cross-country ski construction is the "special cross-country" ski employing balsa wood center laminations or hollow channels to further decrease weight. In some models, the resultant decrease in ski strength is compensated by thin synthetic fiber sheets laminated in the ski's tip, mid-section, and tail. The "Special" ski construction results in a total weight saving of about 500 gr. (about a pound). over conventional cross-country skis. Its lack of overall strength limits the special ski to use over specially-prepared cross-country ski tracks.

Cross-country ski tips have relatively low torsional rigidity, for they must follow terrain bumps without upsetting the balance at the center of the ski. Because in cross-country technique skis may be flat on a snow surface, or lofted to meet a snow surface at angles up to about 45 degrees, cross-country ski tips are turned up more than any other type of ski. The tips are usually extremely soft to achieve maximum forward spring for a given length of ski.

The length of cross-country skis is chosen using the floor-to-wrist-of-upraised-arm rule with the exception that the 210-cm (6 foot, 11 inch) length is the most used. Racers from 175 to 190 cm (5' 9" to 6' 3") in height may well all use 210-cm skis to attain the best combination of tracking and stability on cross-country tracks.

Light-touring Skis use stronger and heavier woods, and may be up to 25% wider than, but otherwise identical in appearance to the cross-country racing ski. Hickory is used for the running-surface to gain strength and durability, at the price of a moderate decrease in wax-holding ability. Compressed beech or sometimes plastic or aluminum is used in the edges. Light touring skis are generally used by serious touring skiers in wooded and rolling terrain, for, unlike cross-country racing skis, their use is not restricted to use in prepared tracks. Although light touring skis are not usually strong enough for trail-breaking through wind-packed snow on high mountain tours, the recent developments in ski construction have produced strong fiberglass and wood models that are becoming increasingly popular with expert mountain and touring skiers. Light-touring skis should be chosen using the floor-to-wrist-of-upraised-arm rule.

General-touring Skis are what most Scandinavians refer to as "skis". The general-touring ski uses the same construction principles, types of wood laminations, and edges as the light-touring ski. The characteristic of a soft tip and a stiff tail are retained, but because the ski is broader and heavier than the light-touring ski, it is not quite as lively. General-touring skis are perhaps the best all-round compromise for the Nordic touring skier. They are light and lively enough to make general touring a pleasure, while strong enough to be used in mountain skiing. They are side-cambered using almost the same profile as used for Alpine skis. Their greater mass allows a camber less than that of a light-touring ski but still greater than that of the yet heavier Alpine ski. Ski mountaineers generally prefer touring skis with plastic or aluminum edges for maximum control on wind-packed or crusty snow. General-touring skis should be chosen using the floor-to-wrist-of-upraised-arm rule.

Mountains Skis are slightly smaller, but have the same general profile as wood Alpine skis. The same materials and construction principles as in the general-touring ski are used. Compressed hardwood or steel edges are used in conjunction with an all-hickory running surface. The forward-spring characteristic is retained to some extent to make the ski liveley, while the tips have a good deal more torsional rigidity then the other Nordic skis. Because of their weight, mountain skis should be used only for high mountain or glacier skiing where breaking trail through wind-pack and crust is necessary. Many Scandinavian skiers have two pairs of Nordic skis: light-touring skis for all-round use, and mountain skis for high-mountain pack trips. Mountain-ski length should be selected according to use; shorter skis are better for steep mountain ranges while longer skis are better for glacier and flatter terrain touring.

BINDINGS

Nordic touring technique requires that the heel be free to lift off the ski. Nordic skis will then use bindings which afford the maximum freedom of foot movement, combined with satisfactory ski control. Seven different models of Nordic binding are compared against a popular toe-and-heel release Alpine binding on page 42. The weights of the various bindings are given in the Table on page 36.

It is worthwhile noting here that the release-type Alpine binding was developed to overcome the dangers inherent in rigidly attaching the foot to the ski with a stiff and inflexible boot-binding combination. Every movement of an Alpine ski is transferred to the firmly-attached foot and leg; every small ski twist is a corresponding leg twist. As shown on page 43, the great flexibility of Nordic boots and bindings, combined with the complete heel freedom, means that there is only a relatively flexible connection between skis and feet. This, combined with the light weight of Nordic equipment makes the Alpine-type release binding unnecessary; Nordic skiing is inherently safer than Alpine skiing.

Several different models of toe bindings for cross-country racing and light touring are available, all share the common design principle that a boot should be attached only at the very tip of the sole in front of the toe. This allows complete freedom of movement; a pair of well broken-in cross-country boots

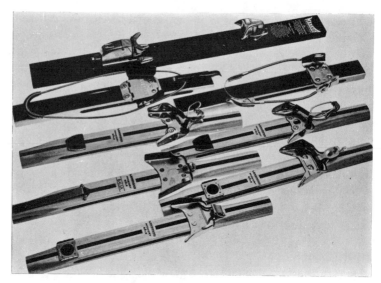

Seven Nordic bindings compared against an Alpine binding; from front to back: "Kloa", "Villom" "Eie", "Rottefella Gold", and "Rottefella Phonix" cross-country and light-touring bindings; "Tempo" and "Kandahar" touring bindings; and "Marker" Alpine binding.

fastened to such bindings are only a little stiffer than tennis shoes. The five bindings shown in the illustration are all made of aluminum and use different mechanisms to hold the boot toe. The "Rottefella" ("Rat Trap") and Villom bindings use bails (spring-metal clamps) to press the welt of the sole down against three pegs projecting upward from the binding base-plate, which mate with corresponding recesses in the boot sole. The "Kloa" ("Claw") binding uses rolled-in ears on the binding side members to hold the boot down, and two spike-like pegs going through small mating holes in the sole welt to attach the boot firmly. The "Eie" binding uses a spring-loaded catch that fits a toe-piece attachment to the boot and thus has no pegs.

Formerly, cross-country bindings were mounted with five to seven screws, and were adjustable to fit the various boot sole widths and side angles. However, boot and binding manufacturers have now standardized on both side angles and widths.

Ski touring boots in bindings are equally as flexible as tennis or jogging shoes.

All boots and bindings now have standard side angles (14° outside, 8.5° inside, as measured from the boot axis.) Boot soles are made with one standard childrens' and three standard adult widths. Binding size is then simply selected to match boot size, and bindings are mounted with three or four screws. This not only simplifies binding mounting, but also results in a stronger mounting and a lesser weakening of the ski.

Because cross-country and light-touring boots are supple, a weighted boot may well twist horizontally when it is held only at its toe. To cure this twisting problem, serrated or U-shaped metal heel plates as shown with the Kloa, Rottefella, and Villom bindings, can be mounted such that they dig into the boot heel when the boot is weighted and flat on the ski. The Eie binding uses a raised metal piece mating with a V-shaped recess in the boot heel for horizontal stability, and can be provided with an accessory spring-steel hook mating with a hitch on the boot heel to fasten the heel down for downhill running.

Cross-Country and light-touring bindings should be used only on cross-country and light-touring skis; they are not strong enough to be used with the heavier ski types. Bindings should be mounted slightly back of the ski's balance point such that when the ski with mounted binding is picked up by the center of the binding ears, the tip will drop downward at an angle of about 20 degrees with the horizontal. Thus, even when the ski is lifted in the cross-country stride, its tip will follow and hold to the snow surface to give maximum ski control.

The general-touring binding comprises a simple toe-iron and cable combination designed for maximum strength while maintaining a reasonable weight. Several models of general-touring bindings are available at present; two of the most popular are shown just in front of the alpine binding on page 42. The upper of the two illustrated has a conventional cable and heel spring, which is usually arranged such that the cable may be hooked into side hitches on touring or mountain skis to tie the heel down for downhill runs. The heel spring may well appear old-fashioned to the modern Alpine skier, for Alpine bindings of thirty years ago used heel springs. In touring technique, the heels lift off the skis, so the binding cables must operate over a range of angles and thus cannot be drawn as tight as on Alpine skis. The front throw incorporates a screw-adjustment or a series of attachment points to provide for length adjustment. The binding illustrated ahead of the Rottefella binding is the "Tempo", a lightweight general-touring binding designed for maximum foot flexibility and reasonable binding strength. It comprises a simple light metal toe iron, with hinged stiff cable bands, and a ratchet type heel clamp. The cables are threaded, and fit into threaded holes in the heel clamp so they may be screwed in or out for length adjustment.

Touring bindings intended for general-touring use should be mounted using the same principle as that for cross-country and light-touring bindings. For high-mountain touring, mount the bindings a little closer to the balance point to make the skis easier to turn on downhill runs.

BOOTS

Three different types of Nordic boot are compared against a typical Alpine boot on p. 45. The four boots pictured are all men's size 41 (U.S. size 8½ - 9). The weights of the boots

From left to right: Light Touring (Kikut, Norway), Cross-Country (Jette, Norway), Touring (Kikut, Norway), and Alpine (Kastinger, Austria) ski boots.

are given in the Table on page 36. Boots should be appropriate to the bindings with which they will be used.

General-touring, or simply "touring" boots are about the same size as hiking or mountain climbing boots, generally are semi-padded, and have a double-tongue or double-lacing arrangement to keep the boot water-tight. The soles are usually made of laminated leather topped by a textured rubber sheet running from toe to heel. Metal plates are attached to the forward edges of the welt to protect the boot where it fits into binding iron. The heels have a single slightly-angled groove for binding cables. General-touring boots are used with both general-touring and mountain skis.

Light-touring boots resemble cross-country boots in shape and size. They use stronger leather in their uppers, have thicker laminated leather or composition soles, and are cut higher (approximately above the ankle) than cross-country boots. Most light-touring boots have a cable groove milled into the heel, so that they can be used with general-touring bindings.

A cross-country boot is cut below the ankle, and resembles an ordinary shoe. Soft and pliable leathers, such as goat or kangaroo skin are used for the uppers to make the boot as supple as a pair of ordinary men's dress shoes. It has a laminated leather or leather-rubber sole which is designed to be flexible under the ball of the foot while simultaneously being strong to withstand

Pull-over socks keep light cross-country boots warm and dry in extreme weather.

side twist. The boot sole is narrow so that the boot will not drag unduly against the snow edges of cross-country ski tracks. The light cross-country boots may not be warm enough in extremely cold weather and can get wet in slushy snow. Rubber or plastic-reinforced stretch nylon pullover socks are available to add insulation and water repellency.

POLES

Nordic poles should be springy to give a little whip which helps push the skier forward much as does the forward spring of Nordic skis. Traditionally, Nordic poles have been made of treated bamboo, to achieve the desired combination of strength, light weight, and liveliness. In the last few years, fiberglass and metal poles have been made with these characteristics.

Most pole baskets have a plastic or metal ring fixed to the pole shaft by a plastic or rubber web. The wrist loops must be adjustable such that the pole swings freely from the hand without danger of being lost. As shown on page 47, the grips have a tapered elliptical cross-section to fit the various hand positions used in touring. In contrast to the straight tips of Alpine poles, the tips of Nordic poles are set at an angle to the pole shaft. This is because the poles are rarely set with a vertical downward thrust, but are swung pendulum-like forward by a forward-swinging arm. The forward-angling pole tips snag on the snow surface to help pole setting and ease pole withdrawal from hard snow.

The correct pole length can be selected by standing with feet together on a flat floor, with the pole vertical, and tip on the floor at one's side. The pole grip should fit snugly under the armpit: a 175 cm (5'9") skier will use poles that are approximately 135 cm (4'5") long. The baskets on cross-country racing poles are usually about 9 cm (3 ½") in diameter, a size suitable for use on packed cross-country racing tracks. The baskets on touring poles are larger, about 11.5 cm (4 ½") in diameter, such that the poles don't sink into deep snow.

The difference between typical Alpine (left) and Nordic (right) pole grips.

From left to right: Treated bamboo touring pole (Eide, Norway), fiberglass touring pole (Eide, Norway), aluminum cross-country pole (Scott, USA), aluminum cross-country pole (Liljedahl, Norway), and aluminum Alpine pole (Kneissel, Austria). Note the larger baskets on the touring poles and the different tips.

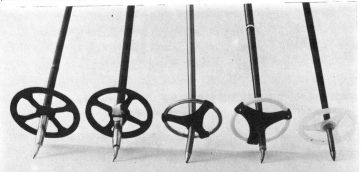

WAXING

Ski touring waxes both grip and glide.

The Why of Waxing

The reason why a waxed ski will both grip and glide is complicated, for snow belongs to the "visco-elastic" class of materials. This means that it has some properties of both viscous fluids (like heavy motor oils and greases) and elastic solids (like rubber). The extent to which each of these properties is present is determined by snow density, crystal type, and temperature. When force is applied to snow, as by a weighted or gliding ski, it may give like rubber, flow like grease, shatter like lump sugar, or react in a combination of these ways. To understand just how wax works on such an apparently unpredictable material as snow, we must look at both snow and wax from a microscopic viewpoint. A microscopic examination of a snow surface reveals many irregularities varying in direction, size, stiffness, and spacing from one another. A similar microscopic examination of a waxed surface shows that the irregularities in the snow penetrate the softer wax to an extent determined by the properties of both snow and wax. If a ski is correctly waxed for touring, small microscopic irregularities and loose particles of the snow surface will penetrate the wax just enough to allow a good "grip" with a motionless weighted ski, yet allow a moving ski that is fully weighted to "glide". A properly waxed ski will glide as long as it is in motion. Once gliding stops, the ski must be unweighted to start it gliding again. In the language of physics, this property is explained by saying that the coefficient of static (non-moving) friction is far greater than the coefficient of dynamic (moving) friction.

From this ideal condition, a ski may be improperly waxed in two directions: "too hard", and "too soft". If the wax is too hard for the snow surface involved, the snow will hardly penetrate the wax at all, and the ski will only glide, and not stand firm when weighted. This is the ideal for Alpine skiing and jumping: to present a surface that appears hard to the type of snow involved. If, on the other hand, the wax used is too soft, then snow particles can penetrate too far into the wax and remain there; the skis will ice up and collect snow.

In addition, the microscopic snow particles' own atmosphere plays an important role. Snow particles lubricated with a water layer will slide over a waxed surface more readily than if they were "dry". The secret of waxing is to determine the nature of the snow surface involved, and then properly apply the right wax.

The difference between static and dynamic friction is what makes touring wax work. Even an unwaxed ski will both grip and glide under ideal conditions. But were it waxed properly, it would both grip and glide better; waxing increases the difference between static and dynamic friction.

Correct waxing then makes skis grip and glide better, and protects them against moisture and wear. A good skier wears out his wax, not his skis.

TYPES OF WAXES

Base Preparation

Unfortunately there are no waxes which both adhere well to bare wood and behave as a touring wax should. Wood ski bottoms must be prepared with compounds which provide a good surface for waxing. These compounds must also seal out water; because wood absorbs water easily, wet skis can ice up and will not hold wax at all. Base preparations can be classified as to their wax-holding and water-sealing abilities. The two general types of base preparations available are impregnating compounds and tars.

Impregnating compound is similar to the creosote used to impregnate the wood pilings used in building piers. It has excellent sealing ability but only minimum wax-holding ability. The liquid should be brushed or sprayed on clean ski bottoms, covering the entire bottom. Most impregnating compounds dry in 8 to 12 hours.

Tars are compounds which are similar to roofing tar. They have good sealing and good wax-holding ability and are the best all-round base preparations. Tars fall into two categories according to application: 1) those which are brushed or sprayed on and air dry, 2) those which are warmed-in. The warm-in treatment is preferred by cross-country racers and long-distance touring skiers, for it provides the best base. It is, however, more difficult, messier, and requires greater care in application than the air-dry treatment. The air-dry tars are applied and let dry in a manner identical to that used for the impregnating com-

raping skis clean,

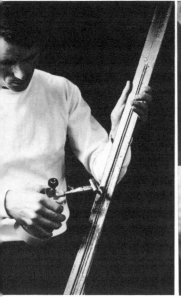

applying,

warming in,

and drying tar are the basic steps in
the warm-in tar base treatment.

pounds. The warm-in tars are brushed evenly over the entire ski bottom, and a blowtorch is run over the surface until the compound bubbles and dries. The blowtorch should be moved continually and not be allowed to play on any one section of the ski long enough to singe or burn the wood. Follow the blowtorch with a rag to remove all excess tar while it is still warm. The result should be a completely dry base. Warming in a tar sometimes increases the camber of cross-country and light-touring skis. To restore the original camber, heat the skis gently on their tops after tarring is finished.

BASE WAXES

Base waxes are similar to the final waxes themselves. They are binders and have excellent wax-holding ability but only minimum sealing ability. Both hard base wax and base klister are available to use "under" final hard waxes and klisters. They should be rubbed or spread on and smoothed out with a waxing cork or a warm waxing iron. They are intended to increase the wax holding ability of skis that have been impregnated or tarred. Cross-country racers often wax for a race under very cold conditions by scraping their skis down to bare wood and warming on a thin layer of solid base wax before applying the final wax. This is because any tar working into the wax will make it a bit slower, but final hard wax will wear off bare wood quickly without some sort of binder.

IMPREG-NATING	TARS			BASE WAXES
	Air-Dry		Warm-in	
	Brush	Aerosol		
Bergendahl Swix Aerosol Östbye Mixol	Bergendahl Haka Rex Suolahden Swix Toko	Karhu Petälä Östbye Swix	Holmenkol Karhu Lasse Back Rode Stjärnglid Suolahden Tento 50 Wallco-Swix	Rex Orange Rode Nera Rode Chola Swix Orange Toko Orange

The choice of base preparation depends on the type of skiing done, and how much effort you are willing to expend.

Unfortunately, the abrasive and fluid properties of snow combine to wear base preparations; a single treatment will not last the life of a pair of skis. There is no fixed rule for how often bases should be treated, except that they must be treated whenever bare wood shows. Usually touring skiers will touch up bare spots whenever necessary and completely treat their skis at least once or twice a season while active cross-country racers may tar-treat and base wax their skis several times a week.

All base preparation methods require that the ski bottoms be clean, dry, and fairly smooth before treatment. The protective coating put on new wood skis at the factory is intended only for storage and transport and should be removed with a scraper and/or sandpaper. Greaseless solvents such as cleaning fluids containing trichloroethylene, gasoline, or turpentine can be used to remove old wax. This sort of cleaning job should be done in the open, as trichloroethylene is highly toxic, and both turpentine and gasoline are flammable. Some special wax removers are available as non-toxic, non-flammable pastes in tubes. Serious touring and cross-country skiers often prefer to use a small blow-torch and a scraper for such cleaning jobs. A scraper followed by sandpaper and sometimes steel wool can be used to polish to a final smooth and level surface. Note: Synthetic-base skis have a permanent base which should not be removed. Waxing torches or irons may damage synthetics, so: *Follow manufacturers' directions for all synthetic bases.*

SELECTING AND APPLYING THE RIGHT WAX

The major job in selecting the right wax for touring is to judge the existing snow conditions. The essential characteristics of snow can be described by the type, size, and wetness of the snow particles. The type and size of snow particles depend on the conditions under which they fell and the stage of the subsequent settling. The wetness of a snow surface is determined by both present and immediately-past snow and air temperatures.

These factors depend on altitude as well. For temperatures below freezing snow surface temperature is usually the same as the still air temperature. At temperatures above freezing, snow temperature may be at or below still-air temperature.

A wax kit can hold all a cross-country skier needs.

Snow can then be classified as being new, settled, or meta-morphosized (modified). In each case it can be dry, wet, or just in the transition or borderline from dry to wet. These classifications are used in the Waxing Table.

Some wax manufacturers and a number of reference books give waxing tables that are based on other identifying features: a common combination is "new" and "old" for snow-particle character and temperatures for snow wetness. The difficulty with such systems is that nobody seems to agree on just how old "old" is and that temperatures are not defined well: They may be snow or air temperatures. Waxing "experts" themselves do not agree on how to judge snow surfaces, although all do agree that some sort of a test should be made. The squeeze-in-gloved-hand and blowing tests are simple guides to judging snow types.

The product lines of the eleven largest touring, and cross-country wax manufacturers are tabulated against the snow types in the Waxing Table on pages 58-59. No two manufacturers produce waxes which are exactly alike, so the listing of waxes opposite one another does not mean they are equal. Approximate temperatures, representing the average of the different manufacturers'

54

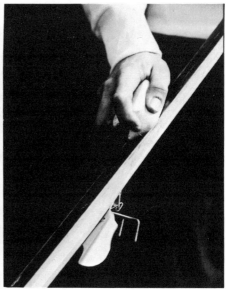

Hard wax is best rubbed on and smoothed out with a waxing cork.

specifications are given *only as a guide*. For exact application information, always follow the individual manufacturer's directions.

The waxes listed fall into three categories: hard waxes, klister waxes, and klisters.*

The hard waxes come in round cans about 3 to 4 cm (about 1 $^1/_2$ in.) in diameter and about 5 cm (2 in.) long. The cans are made either with a thin metal wall which can be peeled off in strips, or with both ends open so the wax can be pushed up as it is used. Hard waxes are best "crayoned" on when the wax itself is cool, and they should be smoothed out with a waxing cork or warm waxing iron.

The klister waxes resemble mixtures of hard waxes and tacky klisters and come in the same cans as do the hard waxes.

* In most Scandinavian languages, special words are used to denote ski waxing in its entire ("skismøring" in Norwegian, "suksivoide" in Finnish and "skidvalla" in Swedish) and the equivalent of the word "wax" ("voks" in Norwegian) is reserved for those ski waxes which actually contain a wax compound. Like "ski" the word "klister" is of Norwegian origin litterally, it means "sticky" in waxing it denotes a paste-like, semi-fluid ski wax used for "warmer" or "older" snow.

Klister is applied warm and smoothed out with a spreader or scraper.

They are generally used for the transition snow conditions. They are best applied when the wax itself is slightly warm, and they can be applied in dabs, and then spread out with a scraper and smoothed with a waxing cork. Some corks are not too good for use on klister waxes, for they crumble easily and leave bits of cork in the wax. For this reason, many seasoned touring skiers and cross-country racers prefer to smooth out klister waxes using the palm of their hand. Otherwise, a small blowtorch can be used for "warming-on."

Klisters are thick fluids and come in tubes of various sizes. They should be applied warm, and should be spread out using a small spreader or scraper. They will hardly flow at all when cold, so it is often necessary to warm a tube before waxing. Waxing corks should not be used with the klisters, because small cork particles will come off and stick in the tacky surface.

All waxes should be applied to a clean, dry, base treated surface, or over the dry surface of a "harder" wax (one for dryer or less settled snow) such that it binds or sticks to the ski and does not rub off rapidly in use. Wax applied to a wet surface or over a softer wax will not last long.

Before a tour, old wax can be removed using the same cleaning methods used to prepare a ski for base treatment with a waxing torch, scraper, or solvents. Unless the manufacturer recommends otherwise, torches and solvents should not be used on synthetic-based skis. Removing old wax is a must if today's conditions are colder than yesterday's. Klister should always be removed after a day's tour.

Many thin layers of wax are far better than a single thick layer. The number of thin layers applied depend somewhat on snow conditions; more layers give more "kick" while fewer layers give more "glide". A tour or track with many uphill stretches requires more "kick" and thus a thicker total wax layer than one in flat terrain which requires more "glide".

The entire running surface should be waxed. The greatest care should be given to the bow of the ski's camber, which is the part of the ski where the difference in weighting between gliding and kicking is most pronounced. It makes absolutely no difference in which direction or directions wax is applied or smoothed out, for it is its microscopic surface and not the directions of any irregularities that determine what it does on snow. Waxed skis should always be allowed to come to outside temperature before they are used; this should *not* be done by placing them base-down in the snow. Wax is porous, and warm wax placed in contact with snow will absorb moisture, which will then freeze and destroy its usefulness. Newly-waxed skis must be given a little time to accomodate to the snow surface involved. Generally, newly-waxes skis will have the right "glide" and "kick" after the first 500 to 1000 meters (550 to 1100 yards) of a tour.

	Snow Type and Characteristics	Temperatures usually are in the range °C	°F	Bratlie Norway	Ex-Elit Sweden	Haka Finland
Falling and New Snow	Extremely Dry (falling powder)	−8° and below	18° and below	Silke (1) (thin layer)	Cold Special (Black)	Vitikelille (602) /Pakaskelille (604)
	Very Dry (powdery: blows easily)	−5° and below	21° and below	Silke (1)	Green	Keskikelille (606)
	Dry (blows with difficulty)	0° to -5°	23° to 32°	Silke (1)	Blue	Leudolle Kelille (608)
	Transition Borderline (clumps in gloved hand)	−1° to +1°	30° to 34°	Blandingsföre (2)	Violet/Red	608 and 610 mixed
	Mushy (rolling snowballs dig in)	0° to +3°	32° to 37°	Klistervoks (3)	Klistervoks	Nouskakelille (610)
	Wet (hand soaking wet after squeezing)	+2° to +6°	35° to 42°	Våt Nysnö Klister (10)	Tö Kristall klister	Uuden klister (700)
Settled Snow	Very Dry (small crystals will blow)	−12° and below	10° and below	Silke (1)	Cold Special/Green	Pakaskelille (604)
	Dry (small crystals will form snowballs)	−1° to −10°	14° to 30°	Grönt Klister (7) (Green)	Blue	Keskikelille (606)/ Leudolle Kelille (608)
	Transition Borderline (large crystals, corns, or clumps)	−1° to +1°	30° to 34°	Blandingsföre (2)/Våt Klister (8) (thin layer)	Red/ Tö Kristall klister	608 and 610 mixed
	Mushy (hand wet after squeezing)	0° to +3°	32° to 37°	Våt Klister (8)	Tö Kristall klister	Nuoskakelille (610)
	Wet (slushy)	+2° to +6°	35° to 42°	Våt Klister (8) (thick layer)	Tö med Tjära klister	Vanhan klister (702)
Metamorphosized Snow ("Skare": Ice, Crust; Pack, Heavy Corn, Slush)	"Skare" — Dry, Hard, Ice, Crust, etc.	−5° and below	21° and below	Skarevoks (4)	Skar Kristall klister	Karkean klister (704)
	Crusty but Softer to Mushy and Wet	−6° to +1°	22° to 34°	Skareklister (9)	Skar Kristall Klister	Vanhan (702) and Karkean (704) klisters mixed
	Wet Slush	0° to +6°	32° to 42°	Våt Klister (8)	Skar Kristall and Tö klisters mixed	Vanhan (704) klisters

Note: Klisters are in tubes, and all other waxes are in cans. Listing under a manufacturer is only a guide. **Read the manufacturer's directions on the can or tube before you wax.**

nkol any	Ostbye Norway	Rex Finland	Rode Italy	Stjärnglid Sweden	Swix Norway	Toko Switzerland	Vauhti Finland
	Special	Turquoise 8571/ Light Green	Light Green	Green	Light Green	Green	Blue (3)
	Mix	Green	Green	Green/Blue	Green	Green	Green (2)
	Mix/Medium	Blue	Blue	66	Blue	Blue	Orange (1)
	Medium/ Klistervox	Violet	Violet	White/ Violet	Violet	Violet	Red (4)
v	Klistervox	Yellow	Yellow	Red	Yellow	Yellow	Red (4)/ Red klister (5)
w r	Klister	Red klister	Red klister	Tö-klister (4)	Yellow klister	Red klister	Red klister (5)
	Special/ Mix	Light Green/ Green	Light Green/ Green	Green	Light Green /Green	Green	Blue (3)/ Green (2)
	Mix	Blue	Blue	Blue/66	Blue	Blue	Green (2)/ Orange (1)
t	Mixolin (klister)/ klistervoks	Violet/ Violet klister	Violet/ Violet klister	White/ Violet klister	Violet	Violet	Red (4)
Red r	Mixoline (klister)	Red/ Red klister	Red/ Red klister	Red/Violet klister	Red/Violet klister	Red/Violet klister	Red klister (5)
er	Klister	Red klister	Silver klister /Red klister	Tö-klister (4 & Kristall)	Red klister	Red klister/ Violet klister	Red klister (5)
er	Mixolinwox/ Skare (klister)	Blue klister	Blue klister/ Red klister	Skar-klister (3 & Kristall)	Blue klister	Blue klister	Blue klister (6)
klisters r er	Mixolinvox/ Mixolin (klister)	Violet klister	Violet klister	Violet klister/ Skar & Tö mixed	Violet klister	Red klister	Blue klister (6)
r klister klister	Klister	Silver and Red klisters mixed	Silver klister	Tö-klister (4 & Kristall)	Red klister (thick layer)	Red klister (thick layer)	Red klister (5) (thick layer)

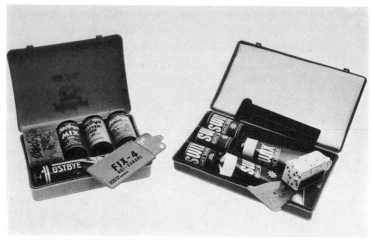

Simplified wax kits for the touring skier.

SIMPLIFIED WAXING

The waxing table is a guide to the best match of wax to snow, and seems to indicate that a large assortment of waxes are necessary. Simplifications can be made if one is not a cross-country racer or high-speed touring skier and can tolerate being a few seconds slower per mile or having to herringbone up the steeper hills. Using one hard wax for dry snow, one soft wax for wet snow, and one for transition conditions is adequate for most touring. Some manufacturers market a three-wax package for just this purpose. With the addition of two klisters, the touring skier can meet all waxing needs.

PROBLEMS

The true test of experience in waxing is the ability to wax for the troublesome transition range and for changing snow conditions.

For transition conditions it is always wise to wax with a thin layer, and then add layers if more "kick" is needed. If the skis still slip backwards, then add softer wax (one for a higher temperature) or a "kicker" in the middle of the camber. When moisture or water penetrates through the wax and into the base of a ski, it will ice up and collect snow. If this occurs, the only way to keep from sticking fast to the snow is to keep

60

moving. Any air space between the ski and the snow surface will only aid the snow-to-ski adhesion, so make an effort to keep the skis flat on and in continuous contact with the snow. The skis should not be lifted at all when going through surface water if the air temperature is below freezing; if possible one should pole through watery stretches on equally weighted skis.

Because different snow conditions require different waxes, changing snow conditions present the greatest waxing problem. The simplest solution is to stop and re-wax for any significant change in snow conditions which makes skiing on the old wax difficult. Cross-country racers are often plagued by changing conditions, for they seldom can take the time to stop to re-wax. The ability to wax for all but the simplest of changing conditions in racing comes only with experience.

WAXING AIDS

The simple combination ski-scraper and waxing-cork is indispensable to the touring skier. The waxing iron is light in weight and fits easily into a parka pocket. Several models of waxing irons are available; one handy type uses fuel tablets to heat the aluminum block of the iron. A pocket waxing thermometer helps judge conditions. A blowtorch is useful for warm-in basewaxing, removing old wax, warming in klisters, drying wet skis before waxing, or for quickly heating a waxing iron. Three types of blowtorch are presently popular: small self-pressurizing, white-gasoline torches. butane cartridge, and propane-tank torches. The gasoline torches are the cheapest, whereas the gas torches are easier to light and put out more heat for their weight*. Special wax-dissolving hand cleaners and some mechanic's water-less hand cleaners will remove wax from hands or clothing. Ordinary vaseline is a good solvent for klisters.

* Light-weight, disposable gas cartridges contain liquid butane, which freezes at 30° to 31°F. Liquid propane freezes at -44°F, but exerts too much pressure to be put in cartridges and must be put in stronger, heavier tanks. For all practical purposes, the two gases burn equally well at room temperature. For touring in sub-freezing weather, the choice is between a heavier propane torch which can always be lit and a lighter butane torch which must be insulated or warmed.

Waxing torches, from left to right: "Gaz" butane- cartridge torch, "Sievert" propane-tank torch, "Primus" butane-cartridge torch. The Gaz and Sievert torches are fitted with waxing-iron attachments.

Natural and synthetic waxing, corks, scrapers, combined scraper-corks, waxing iron, and waxing thermometer.

Removing hard wax.   Removing klister.

STORING SKIS

Wax left on skis hardens with time and becomes difficult to remove. Skis must be cleaned before being stored for any extended period, but they should not be stored with their running surfaces cleaned to bare wood. They should be base treated either with impregnating compound or tar, and carefully dried. Paraffin wax can be used on any other exposed wood scratches. The rule for storage is the same as for using skis: *Keep Moisture Out!* Aside from direct destructive breaks, nothing ruins skis faster than letting them absorb moisture at any time during use or storage. Skis well protected can be used directly next season with no further preparation.

Well-prepared modern laminated skis have another advantage over their predecessors: they retain their camber while stored no matter whether they are laid flat, stood on end, or tied or bound in any manner. They can be simply stood in a corner or in a closet.

Excessive camber can be reduced in storage by strapping a pair of skis together at their mid points, and gently but thoroughly heating their top sides before storage.

Deficient camber is difficult to correct. Blocking skis, as was common practice some 20 to 30 years ago, will only distort the tips and tails. The best method of increasing camber is to heat the skis thoroughly in the middle of their running surfaces before storage.

The tips and tails of laminated skis can easily be altered by warming both top an bottom surfaces, and gently bending as required. Warped tails, as often caused by absorbed moisture, absorbed when the skis stand in puddles of melted snow. can be corrected in this manner.

A FINAL TIP

The greatest secret in successful touring waxing is experience with the waxes you use. Pick one manufacturer's series of waxes and learn their characteristics under use. After some experience you will be able to look at a snowy mountain side, squeeze a bit of snow in your hand, and pick out a suitable wax.

CLOTHING AND EQUIPMENT

In ski touring clothing, packs, and equipment the word is lightweight.

This is a book on what is different about Nordic touring. No attempt will be made to beleaguer the reader with complete clothing information, for the literature of skiing, mountaineering, and other outdoor activities is full of advice on how to dress warmly for cold weather. Against this wealth of information, only a few important hints will be given here.

Muscles generate heat, which may be more efficiently trapped by using more insulation, or more can be produced by more muscle contraction. This means that there are two basic ways

65

Several light clothing layers insulate better than a single heavy layer. From left to right: fine weave long underwear and mesh shirt form the first layer, socks over the knees and a turtle-neck tne second, and a stretch nylon two-piece touring suit and boots the third (touring suit and socks courtesy of Norge-Ski, boots courtesy of Kikut)

to stay warm in cold weather: insulate the body with more clothing or keep moving. The more motion involved in an activity, the less clothing required and vice versa. This is because about three-quarters of the energy the body produces is in the form of heat; only a quarter goes to direct physical movement. Tests made on cross-country racers have often shown that they have body temperatures of 39°C (102°F) immediately after finishing a 50-km race. Although the touring skier does not move as fast and does not get as warm as the cross-country racer, his motion keeps him far warmer than he would be were he skiing only downhill. Touring and cross-country clothing must allow ventilation yet be wind-resistant. Like other winter outdoor clothing, it should be slightly water-repellent.

The down-filled or padded parka is usually too warm for all but the coldest high-mountain tours. A single or double shell parka or "anorak" over a sweater is warm enough and pro-

Warm-up suits go over other clothing and can be put on with skis on (suit courtesy of Odlo).

vides adequate ventilation for most touring needs. Cross-country racers seldom wear more than long underwear plus a stretch pull-over and occasionally a nylon wind shirt.

Knickers and knee-socks are preferred for touring, because they allow complete leg and knee freedom in the various strides. Stretch pants are unadvisable because they partially hinder leg movement and create a slight extra resistance for legs to work against. The slight extra resistance per step may not be much, but added up over a day's tour, it can be appreciable. Single- and double-layer wind-resistant knickers are the most useful for

A well-fitting frame rucksack is ideal for ski touring.

all-round touring. Cross-country racers and light-touring skiers often use stretch knickers made of a heavy stretch material similar to that used in gymnastic clothes. For extended high-mountain tours, slightly loose full-length ski pants or full-length nylon wind resistant over-pants put on over knickers are often used.

Matching sets of anorak or parka and knickers in wind-resistant synthetic-blend fabric are as attractive as they are practical. Cross-country racing teams and some ski touring clubs often choose matching or complementary stretch blouse-and-knickers sets as a team uniform.

Caps and gloves or mittens are as necessary for touring as for any other winter sport activity. An otherwise fully-clothed skier

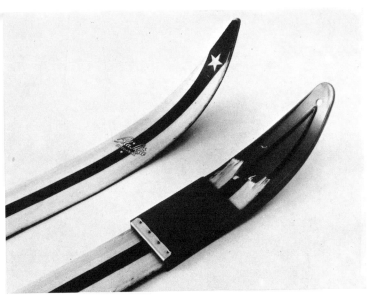

A spare tip is a must for long tours.

may lose as much as 20% of his total produced body heat through his hands and another 20% through his scalp.

Most parka pockets are roomy, but they have their limits. For extended tours, a pack is necessary. A ski touring pack must fit the back well so as not to affect body balance. It must allow full, free arm movement, and place the carried weight close in to the body where it will not upset a skier on downhill runs or turns. The frame rucksack is the best pack for ski touring of all the types of packs available. Packboards and packframes are ideal for touring on foot, but their loaded centers of weight are too high for ski touring. Small frameless packs are ideal for shorter day tours, but are cumbersome when loaded with the equipment necessary for an extended tour.

In addition to wax, clothing, food and camping equipment, the careful touring skier needs a few items beyond those needed for a foot hike. If they break, touring skis usally break at the tip, so a spare tip or tip clamp is a must for longer tours. A small tool kit containing a pair of pliers, a screw driver, an awl, screws, tape, and brass wire will enable you to make almost any repair needed.

CROSS-COUNTRY

Cross-country ski racing is unique among athletic events (1971 Holmen-kollen women's relay).

Cross-country ski racing is unique among athletic events. Its shortest international race distance, 5 kilometers (about 3 miles), is one of the long-distance events in track. It is performed on skis, yet it requires athletic abilities decidedly different from those for any other skiing event. No other athletic event requires the use of so many body muscles over such long periods of time; physiological tests have shown cross-country racers to be the most superbly conditioned of all athletes.

Often mere seconds separate the medal winners from each other in races lasting several hours. The 1970 FIS 50 kilometer race was typical: the top three places were all timed at about 2 hours and 50 minutes, but only eight seconds separated the silver and bronze medal winners. Eight seconds over a distance of 31 miles, for racers who started separately, three and a half minutes apart, and never saw each other during the course of the race! Where did that 8 seconds go? Any seemingly minor waste motion in his stride would have been repeated thousands of times over 50 km. Would 2 layers of special green wax have been better than one layer of regular green? A moment's hesitation in a high-speed turn could catch a tip, losing speed, energy, and time. Was it a little extra gulp at the feeding station, or could it have been passing a feeding station and suffering a slow down later? A dull pole tip could cause a slip on a steep icy hill, at best a break in rhythm, at worst a fall. Eight seconds? Eight double poles too few over 31 miles? The possibilities are endless. Or maybe he had just planned the race wrong; at 40 km he had been in first place.

More than any other event, cross country ski racing requires the racer to plan, judge, and compete against himself.

TECHNIQUE

The secret of cross-country skiing lies chiefly in a stride technique that has matured steadily through the years. As in many other sports, this technique has come to a peak of technical progress since World War II. Modern equipment has greatly aided this development: the cross-country equipment used in the 1970 FIS World Championships weighed less than half as much as the equivalent equipment used twenty years earlier.

A tense anchor relay
and a happy gold me(
(1968 Winter Olympic
women's relay).

Cross-country racing is rhythmic movement; there is no substitute for seeing it done first-hand. A book or an illustration is not alive: it can tell you but it can not show you how to race. Only the more important cross-country details will be given here; with these in mind, *go watch a race*.

The sequence illustrations on pages 18 through 33 are a guide to cross-country technique. The basic difference between good cross-country technique and good touring technique is the rapidity of the movements and the explosive force put into each leg kick and each arm movement. Technique in cross-country skiing is thus made up of a series of explosive and effective movements blending into a rhythmic whole. Endurance is the key to winning. But technique and endurance are dependent on one another. If your technique is good, you last longer. If your endurance is poor, you tire quickly and your technique gets poor, which just tires you out more.

From a physical viewpoint, the single aim of cross-country technique is forward speed. Rapid arm and leg movements are of little use if they do not result in a correspondingly high forward speed. Any movement that does not result in forward speed is unwanted, no matter how small it may be. Every movement the body makes uses up energy, and wasted movement is wasted energy, and wasted energy is a lower speed.

Any age is right for cross-country racing.

Modern cross-country technique can best be described as having a "neutral" body position. Older cross-country technique was characterized by a side-to-side motion as the skier placed his weight directly over one ski and then the other. Modern understanding of ski principles and lighter equipment have produced a more natural technique. No longer do skiers stand over a ski to weight it prior to the kick or during the gliding phase; they spring towards the ski, flex, and rebound. Dynamically the weight is on the ski, but the body appears to "hang" almost neutrally between the skis.

This neutral body position is the one which allows the longest and most natural rest periods between the arm and leg movements that give forward speed. "Explode-relax-explode-relax" is working order for cross-country muscles. The pole is swung forward; it is not whipped forward. The leg moves actively but it is not kicked forward. As in touring, these forward movements are pendulum-like. But unlike in touring, in cross-country racing they must be active and not passive movements. The energy put into each forward movement depends on the skier's speed and length of the race. Today's skiers have powerful, active forward movements on all steep uphills and to a lesser degree on all gradual uphills. They drive forward at the start of each kick of the diagonal stride on the flat and they possess the physical condition to maintain this drive even in the 30 km and 50 km races. Like runners, they can sprint by speeding up these forward movements. Hips are not fixed, but are rotated about a central axis, not swung from the axis. A backward-swinging leg draws its hip along. The forward-rotating hip swings the leg forward. In Alpine skiing, arms are away from the body. In cross-country they are close in. Moving them in and out or back and forth in front of the body wastes energy. An arm out from the body can't pull or push on a pole as effectively or as powerfully as one close in to the body. An arm close in to the body takes less muscle power to swing forward than one further out. Arms work parallel to the track; their job is to push the skier forward, not from side to side. The neutral energy-conserving body position and the various swing phases are the keys to good cross-country technique. Maintaining good technique in a race is, in turn, critically dependent on physical training.

Odd Martinsen of Norway (skiing the 1970 FIS 15 km race) shows the modern relaxed style with a neutral body position. All movement is directed along the track. Notice arms close in, shoulders over poles, and general body drive.

Training for cross-country is best done in terrain similar to that used for races (Sundsvall, Sweden).

TRAINING

Training for cross-country skiing is aimed at building up the necessary abilities for racing plus those abilities unique to good technique. More than any other single factor, better training knowledge and superior physical training are responsible for today's skiers being faster than those of yesteryear. Generally speaking, a cross-country skier follows much the same year-round

76

training as that used by long-distance and cross-country foot runners, with the addition of special skiing exercises and movements. But training for cross-country skiing is not easily regimented. Race-course profiles are seldom identical, and the terrain variations encountered make it impossible to single out any one unique required strength or ability. The physiological abilities required are aerobic capacity, or the ability to work when supplied with oxygen, and anaerobic capacity, or the ability to work with an oxygen debt. This is because cross-country skiing is mostly an endurance event requiring considerable aerobic capacity, but it also has many anaerobic periods, such as when a racer runs a hill or sprints in a relay finish. The training necessary to produce these capabilities and those necessary to ski well technically can be divided up into distance, interval, tempo, and strength training.

Distance training is a continuous pace, foot running or skiing of at least half and usually not more than one-and-a-half times the duration of a ski race. Its purpose is to build up aerobic capacity.

Interval training is a skiing stride, foot- or skiing-run comprising a series of intense but relatively short work periods separated from one another by rest intervals of shorter duration. Its purpose is to build up anaerobic capacity, and provide the ability to tolerate the transition from aerobic to anaerobic. The Swedish training program divides interval training into three types as shown in the table below.

Type	Duration	Rest Period	Repetitions
Long intervals	3-4 min. up to 8 min.	2-3 min. up to 5 min.	2-10 times maximum 8 times
Short intervals "15-15" intervals	70 seconds 15 seconds	20 seconds 15 seconds	4-16 times 20-60 times, can be divided in 3 periods of 20 times each

Three types of interval training useful in cross-country training.

Tempo training is training designed to enable a skier to maintain the high speed required in a race. Physiologically, its purpose is to enable the body to tolerate high lactic acid concentrations over longer periods of time. It consists of foot-running or skiing at racing speed for a period equal to ten to twenty percent of the race's duration. Activity periods can be repeated several times with long rests between. The duration of activity depends on the terrain and speed involved. You should feel slightly stiff at the end of each work period. This stiffness is one sign of high lactic acid concentration. Some top skiers who race several times a week use shorter races as tempo training for longer and often more important races.

Strength training is designed to build up the required strengths in the different movement patterns necessary to master competitive technique. All strength training should be done with cross-country in mind. Extremely powerful muscles capable of slowly exerting great force are useless for cross-country skiing where rapid, explosive movements are needed. Weight training is valuable to strengthen weak muscles. The total weight used in regular workouts should be limited by what you can still move with the same rapid explosive movements as in skiing. A rule-of-the-thumb for maximum weight is: for leg training use maximum weight of 40% body weight. Other resistances such as body weight (as with push-ups and pull-ups) or terrain (as in running up steep hills or on soft ground) can be used. Regular but less-frequent work-outs with heavier weights and fewer repetitions are useful to build up weak muscle groups or to maintain maximum strength.

Testing. The true test of effective training is improved skiing times. However, physiological testing is useful during a training season as a check. Many tests are in use, of which the Ergometer cycle is perhaps the most reliable and easily administered. In the Ergometer test, the subject pedals a stationary cycle at a constant speed against a resistance. The measured pulse rate and body weight then give an index of the maximal oxygen uptake, which is the most important physiological factor in conditioning for cross-country skiing. Ergometer cycles are standard team equipment for most major cross-country teams.

Space does not permit giving a complete training program here.

Ergometer cycles test maximal aerobic power, the single most important factor of a racer's conditioning (US Nordic team training camp).

As a guide, an outline of the four training seasons as given in the Norwegian men's cross-country training manual is given below. The monthly amounts of training and types of training are shown in the chart on page 80.

May, June, July: Stay in shape. Distance training dominates, occupying about three-quarters of training time. Interval training account for a little under a quarter, and increases towards the end of the period. Do a little strength training, working on any specially weak muscles. Three-four training days per week.

August, September, October: Buildup. At the beginning, distance training occupies the greater part of the program, but at the end interval training accounts for almost half. Tempo training begins in November. In August, train four-five days a week. In September and October, train five-six days a week.

November, December: Change over. This is the transition period when the body has to become accustomed to skiing. The emphasis is on special ski training. Distance and interval training continue, but tempo and on-ski technique training become increasingly more important. Train initially six days a week, and then cut back to five after the race season starts.

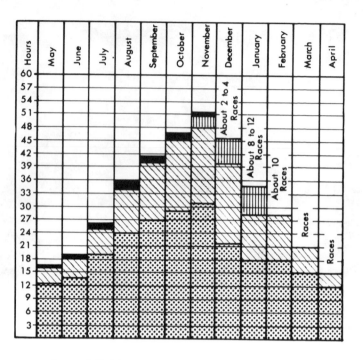

Types of Training:

| | DISTANCE | | TEMPO |
| | INTERVAL | | MISC. (Strength, Special, etc.) |

The Norwegian men's training program (courtesy of Norwegian Ski Federation).

January, February, March, April: Racing. Initially an average of two races a week, often more towards the end of the period. Distance and interval training continue in an amount suited to individual condition and racing schedules. Tempo training is gradually phased out. Train about four days a week.

The amount and intensity of training for men is, of course, considerably more than that reasonable or necessary for boys, girls, or women, simply because they race shorter distances. As an approximate guide, top women cross-country skiers seldom train more than two-thirds as much distance in training. Boys and girls will train correspondingly less.

Arm exercises with weights and pulleys or elastic cords are excellent off-season training.

Because skiing uses both arms and legs, while track uses only legs, a skiing training program is similar to a track training program with the addition of special arm training. Arm strength training uses pulleys, ropes and weights or large elastic bands (bicycle innertubes are fine) for building up poling muscles.

The pulleys or elastics should be fastened well above shoulder height to get the correct angle of pull. Note that this is strength training and does not duplicate pole movements exactly. In poling, the resistance is greatest in the initial pull phase and then decreases to almost nothing at the end of the push phase. Elastics give an increasing resistance, which is just the opposite of the poling resistance pattern. Weights on pulleys give constant resistance, which more closely approximates pole movements.

IMITATION TRAINING

Training specifically to work skiing muscles in the same motions and body joints in the same angles as in skiing is imitation training. Two imitation training exercises have recently come into widespread use: roller skiing and uphill ski striding.

Roller skis are small wheeled platforms attached to the foot with standard cross-country bindings and boots. The wheels are fitted with ratchets such that the skis cannot roll backwards. The skis should usually be used on paved surfaces using poles about the same length as used on snow. Almost all cross-country movements can be done on roller skis, but they are most useful for training for the diagonal stride and double poling, the movements otherwise lacking in summer training.

The dry-land ski-stride is done uphill to provide the necessary

The kick is short and explosive, and arms are duplicating diagonal stride movements. Compare this position with the third photo in the diagonal-stride sequence on page 18.

The left pole is pushing, th right pole is swinging forwar and the kick is just starting o the right foot. Compare with t sixth photo in the diagona stride sequence on page 19.

The right pole is pushing, the left pole is swinging forward, and the kick is just starting on the left foot. This is the opposite of the second picture.

The runner is completely in the air for an instant as the kick finishes.

resistance, and can be done at a fast walk or a bounding run. It can be done without or with poles. and, because it is done in the same terrain as used for skiing, it drills in correct movement patterns and builds up a sense for terrain. The most important features are a rapid and complete leg extension with each kick, and good rhythm and balance. The bounding-run version with poles is illustrated here.

Roller skis are most often used for imitation training of double poling and diagonal stride movements.

TRAINING PROGRAMS

The training principles and methods described here are the bases for training programs but are not complete descriptions of year-round programs. Concise training programs are available from the offices of the national ski associations of countries participating in the Nordic events. These programs are an exacting guide to training and competition for the serious cross-country racer and are usually available simply by request, from your national ski association.

COURSES AND REGULATIONS

Standard international cross-country course lengths vary from 5 km (3.1 miles) to 50 km (31 miles). Courses are laid out in rolling terrain with climbs, downhills, turns, and flat stretches to challenge the skiers' technique, condition, and tactics. A terrain profile of a course gives an idea of its difficulty.

A cross-country course laid out and maintained according to the international FIS (International Ski Federation) specifications, allows the skiers to put their abilities to test at the international level. The complete FIS regulations are too lengthy to

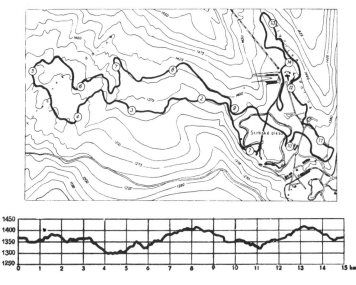

Typical course: The 1970 FIS men's 15 km race course profile, Vysoké Tatry, Czechoslovakia. Elevations in meters.

85

repeat here; they are available from the various national ski associations.

The maximum permissible lengths of races in most countries depend on the skiers' ages and sex shown in the table. As of the 1971 FIS Ski Congress in Opatija, the FIS removed the age limit for cross-country participants in World Ski Championships. The national ski associations are responsible for the perfect preparation of their racers.

Age as of January 1	Class	Maximum Race Length
Men		
21 and over	Senior	FIS 50 km, otherwise not limited
20	Senior	20 km
18 and 19	Junior	15 km
16 and 17	Younger Junior	10 km, age classes
14 and 15	Older Boys	5 km, age classes
12 and 13	Younger Boys	3 km, age classes
11 and under	Small Boys	2 km, age classes
Women		FIS 10 km, otherwise 35 km
18 and over	Senior	touring
16 and 17	Junior	5 km, age classes
14 and 15	Older Girls	5 km, age classes
12 and 13	Younger Girls	3 km, age classes
11 and under	Small Girls	2 km, age classes

Cross-Country race lengths usually depend on age

Course difficulty can be defined in terms of the total amount of climbing, or total elevation gain, in the entire course. The standards for elevation gain are:

Course	Total elevation gain Normally in the range	Typical course: 1970 FIS World Championships
5-km women's	150— 200 m (492— 656 ft)	142 m (462 ft)
10-km women's	250— 350 m (820—1150 ft)	349 m (1142 ft)
10-km men's	300— 450 m (984—1475 ft)	375 m (1230 ft)
15-km men's	450— 600 m (1475—1965 ft)	553 m (1810 ft)
30-km men's	750—1000 m (2480—3280 ft)	1026 m (3360 ft)
50-km men's	1200—1500 m (3940—4920 ft)	1770 m (5800 ft)

Up until 1971, the FIS maximum elevation for a course was 1500 meters (4920 ft.) above sea level. Courses at higher elevations could be granted special approval by the FIS cross-country committee. As of 1971, the maximum permissible FIS elevation is 1650 meters (5400 ft.) above sea level with no permission possible for higher elevations. The 1972 Sapporo and 1976 Denver Winter Olympics are excepted, as their sites were approved before the ruling was made.

The relay is cross-country's "sprint" event (1970 FIS World Championships, Vysoké Tatry, Czechoslovakia).

Relays, combined cross-country, and biathlon complete the list of cross-country events.

Relays: Men's relays are 3 x 10 km or 4 x 10 km and women's are 3 x 5 km. As of the 1974 World Ski Championships, the standard FIS women's relay will be 4 x 5 km. Total elevation gains are the same as for single-race courses of same length. The course should preferably be laid out with two tracks: this is compulsory for the final 500 meters (550 yards).

Combined: The cross-country course for the Nordic combined is 15 km long, and has the same general specifications as for the 15 km special course.

Biathlon: The individual biathlon event comprises 4 shooting bouts on a 20 km cross-country course, while the 4-man relay comprises 2 shooting bouts on each of its 4 legs. Courses are often laid out in loops using a single common range for all shooting.

On 20 kilometer and longer races, the racers must "feed", or replenish carbohydrates used and liquids lost. Warm fruit or berry juice drinks containing about ten percent dextrose are best

Cross-country tracks can be easily made using a track sled towed behind a snow scooter (photo courtesy Spår-Kalle, Sweden).

for race feeding stations. "Stocking up" on glucose by eating large quantities of food or drinking high dextrose drinks just before a race has little or no beneficial effect. It may, if carried to extremes, be detrimental. If the amount consumed is enough to increase the blood glucose level, normally about 1 gram per liter (about 0.1%), the pancreas may counteract and produce enough insulin to cause insulin shock - literally, a sugar deficiency. In other words, too much sugar before a race can rob the body of sugar during the race.

WHO ME?

The lure of mountain touring or the call of the cross-country track as shown by Babben Enger Damon (gold in 1968 Winter Olympics relay), all belong . . .

Anyone can enjoy ski touring. A large back yard becomes a ski area for tots who can begin to learn touring technique not long after they have learned to walk. A snow-covered golf-course or frozen lake is an ideal winter playground for youngsters with touring skis. For the price of a single pair of good Alpine skis, the athletically-inclined youngster can buy a complete set of the best cross-country racing equipment. Any young athlete who excels in track events in summer and enjoys winter sports should be encouraged to take up cross-country skiing. For the adult novice who is understandably cautious about taking up Alpine skiing because of the cost and danger, Nordic touring offers a way to enjoy skiing on the nearest snow patch. For the handicapped, Nordic touring is the key to enjoying a winter recreational and sporting activity. In Norway, the annual "Rid-der-rennet" ("Race of the Knights") cross-country race attracts hundreds of blind and disabled skiers from all over the world.

And for the winter visitor to the Nordic countries, touring skiing is a must; nowhere in the world is Nordic touring more thoroughly a part of life. Winter weekends often find Norwegian or Finnish cities empty and lonely from dawn to dusk while a sizable portion of their population is out skiing. A foreigner visiting Norway in the early spring may have forgotten snow for the year, but if he should arrive the week before Easter Sunday, he would soon discover that the Norwegians haven't. Cities and towns the country over shrivel to less than half their normal population for the Easter week, as school, shop, parliament and palace doors close and the population swarms to the mountains to ski during the traditional "Påske" week.

But even to the skiing novice, Nordic touring is ideal in that it is basically easier than Alpine downhill to master to the point where it can be enjoyed. No matter what his final goal, the skiing novice's first few encounters with skis are made easier if he can do something on skis he has done before: walk. He soon finds that he can control his skis, and that there are no terrors to sliding. He does not stand still, but he moves around and quickly becomes acclimated to the brisk outdoor weather.

In the Alpine-oriented countries, introductory touring could well take the place of today's traumatic (and expensive) rush to get on the hill. Where Nordic touring made the introduction

Erling Stordahl (no. 61) and his seeing-eye running mate cross the finish line of Norway's annual "Ridderrennet" cross-country race for blind and disabled skiers. Stordahl is Ridderrennet's founder.

If you don't have snow, make it (Annual pre-season cross-country, Kongsvinger, Norway county fair).

to all skiing, it would not be surprising if more skiers stayed with the sport.

And for those who will never really like Alpine downhill skiing, here is a chance to avoid becoming a non-skier, that most dreadful of all fates.

Enjoy your touring . . .

Photo and Illustration Credits: M.M. Brady: 9, 15, 21, 68, 72, 73, 75, 76, 79, 87, 88, 89, 92; Studio 9: 11; S. Sövik: 20; L. Skogen: 38; Norwegian Ski Federation: 80; Czechoslovak Ski Federation: 85; Spår-Kalle AB: 88; Pedro: 93. Otherwise all photography by Frits Solvang.